LOCKDOWN MUSINGS

BIDYUT BARAN SEN

Inkfeathers Publishing
www.inkfeathers.com

Lockdown Musings
by Bidyut Baran Sen
Paperback Edition

First Published in India in 2022
by Inkfeathers Publishing, New Delhi 110095
Edited by Ayush Aggarwal

ISBN 9789390882304

www.inkfeathers.com

Dedicated to

All my friends from Literature lovers group,
my classmates, Prabasi Bangabandhus and
my family members who have encouraged me
to take my writings to publishing end.

Contents

Foreword

> "Two things fill the mind with ever new and increasing admiration and awe, the more often and steadily we reflect upon them: the starry heavens above and the moral law within."
>
> —Immanuel Kant

The pandemic did different things for different people. From some it snatched the loves of their lives; for many, there was misery and hardship; for most, it was a multitude of inconveniences. But for all, it was a series of lessons to be learned the hard way. The future will tell whether we have learnt or not.

But there were a few for whom it was an opportunity in disguise. They used their time to deeply reflect upon the meaning of life and the world and give expression to their thoughts in a way as beautiful as the nature around us. Bidyut Baran Sen is one such person. He is the brightest star of our Literature Lovers group, and like Immanuel Kant, can be described as both a wanderer of the earth as well as an explorer of the mind, both as a romantic as well as a mystic. For how else to describe a person who tells a kite "it carries his soul to the sky" or who "made her the prisoner of his beliefs and lost her very soon" or who finally finds the "lost key"?

In "Lockdown Musings", he offers a bouquet of beautiful flowers whose fragrance never fades once smelt.

In "Lockdown Musings", he unlocks his soul.

Poetry, as Rita Dove says, is "language at its most distilled and most powerful". It is a call of the soul, a yearning that adds meaning to all the din of daily life. It is therapeutic for the tormented soul and even a 'prescription' for heart aches from a heart doctor like me! It soothes our nerves and pacifies our hearts. Please take it. Don't fear that it is only fifty plus pages and that the experience will get over fast; for though it is a book you can finish in an evening, it is one which can be read, reread, and savoured over a lifetime. A thing of beauty is a joy forever. May the joy begin.

—Dr Akshay Mehta

Interventional Cardiologist

Founder of 'Literature Lovers Club', Mumbai

Author's Note

I have been out of touch from my poetry writing since I joined my professional career as Chemical Engineer after leaving Jadavpur University, which was like a flowering pot for all the young aspirant poetry writers.

We had the eminent poets like Sankha Ghosh, Pabitra Sarkar and Alokeranjan Dasgupta as teachers. When we turned to sympathize with the Socialist movement, Subhas Mukhopadhayay also inspired us. We got opportunities to interact with Sunil Gangopadhyay, Shakti Chattopdhayay, Ratneswar Hazra, Dinesh Das and many others. That environment could have turned us to real poets, but unfortunately, we were not with great poetic material. It was a good decision not to follow the profession, where possibly, we could do a little. But the flavour of poetry did not leave me altogether. My Himalayan treks also helped to pen down my experiences in brief with few short stories on the journey. Reading has been a passion always and some lines trickling out of pen continued.

Pandemic brought a situation converting us to prisoners in our own cells, but with plenty of fresh air, unlike solitary jails. We all could pursue some passion of our own liking and that brought my ink-flow back in my pen in form of poetry. These are more of sharing my experiences during my journey of life and pandemic. My success will be judged by whether these writing have touched the readers' mind some where some time.

I am grateful to Dr Akshay Mehta, a renowned interventional cardiologist and a well-known author of the book 'Romancing the Heart', who is also an inspiration behind our 'Literature Lovers' group in Mumbai, for his lovely foreword which aptly describes his love for literature.

I am also grateful to Miss Uma Bokil of Inkfeathers Publishing and the back-up team for relentlessly helping me in editing the poems on my first publishing effort.

Bidyut Baran Sen

15th August 2021

Walking Alone

Walking alone for a long time now
Crossed many continents, oceans and mountains.
Meeting many a different face in my journey
Some strong grips of childhood lost forever,
Some of the them are loosely bonded
Some grips came along the way in youth,
And then came the strongest grip of a soft tiny hand
Holding on with complete trust in me;
Will be loose and lost again
On my way to final journey,
To reach the final truth
Of walking alone.

"And the light shineth in the darkness
And the darkness comprehended it not (John 1.5)"

Covid 19

Hello, my friend dressed in darkness
with an ugly beauty of an unknown,
Embracing us with quiet passion
to show our worth.

Cleaned my hand
Cleaned my body
Cleaned my outer dress;
Will I be able to clean the inner self!
Will I be able to clean the outer world!

Covid 19
Come with your friends
Come with your full force
Come and clean me from inside out and around me,
When the morning glow shines after the dark night,
I shall see a beautiful sunlight.

Pure as it was
When the earth came out of mother's womb,
When the amoeba came in to form
When the DNA was born,
When the creation named man
Looked at the sky for first time.

I see a beautiful day and the night
As serene as it could be,
Before I walk towards the Moon
And the Sun.

On The Sea Shore

Walking on the seashore trying to leave my footprint–
Some were light and some were deep,
Called the sky with pride and glory
Look at them,
Then the tides came
Footprints were nowhere to be seen.

Made an elegant castle on the shore
With sand at bottom and sand on top
A galaxy of rooms and stairs,
With countless windows and doors,
Could not count any
When the tidal waves came
My castle was nowhere to be seen.

The sun shines and fades out
Its candescent light mellows down,
Shadow of a gloomy night looms ahead
Sky is cloudy to will there be rain?
I am still at seashore
Looking for the marks on the sand.

From My Balcony

I look at the road
There is hardly any one nowadays,
Absent are the buses, the cars
and the motorbikes wheezing us by.
The market on both side of the roads
Observing eerie silence with shutters down,
In reminiscing of some one
with a crown on the head.

A man prancing around, looking for someone
He finds the vendor at the corner
carrying vegetables and fruits in the cart,
Does not allow the man to touch any
Offering a plastic bag on a basket
And taking the money in a bowl.

Days are muted and night follows
With the hush of graveyard,
When the ghost rules the earth with its law
All the houses around watches in silent mourning.

When the new sun rises
With a brighter light reflecting on us,
With pure air around
With birds chirping on the trees,
With the fresh green leaves
New ideas will be born,
New hearts will replace the older ones
With smiles of new born children.

I patiently wait for that day, my Lord!

Sea Gull

Hey, Seagull,
Where do you all go?
High in the sky with no limit to fly
With wings open dancing in the air,
Like waves in the ocean below.

Hey, Seagull,
Will you take me with you?
Far away from my theatre room
where I appear day and night.
With make up on my face,
adding no value to my life.
When children die in hunger
Liberia, Burundi, Congo or Niger,
Where people die in hatred
Name any place and demon is there.
Like a clown, I go around
In a make-believe role,
With clapping from people around me.

Hey, Seagull,
Take me to a place of eternal bliss,
Where each one celebrates life
Where smile is pure as ever
Like a new born child.

Hey, Seagull,
Bless me to be reborn
as a baby to a Seagull like you.

To A Dear Friend

An enigma of woman empowered with freedom
from bondages of every nature
Why care for any norm?
There is nothing bigger than universal truth
The omnipresent one—the sublime almighty.
This is me—take it or leave it.

I could be a normal human like all
24 by 7 housewife managing routine ritual,
Puja path, exercise, daily soaps on the TV
Candy crush and weekly kitties
I could be shy to elders with a veil on my head
Touching the feet of the elderly
Without knowing their vices and habits
A mother to the core taking care of children,
Even when they become bigger
Or waiting for husband to come home all life,
To serve him the flavour of home.

Alas!
That's not in my blood
As I know for sure,
Nothing belongs to me.
I don't belong to any one
I could be a photo frame tomorrow,
With a garland on me,
The only father, husband and son I have
Is thee—the ultimate to whom I submit.

Otherwise
I am me, that's all!
Take it or leave it.

Amazon

From the time I heard about you
From the time I set my foot near you
You made my blood flow high,
Like when you think of your dear ones
And the moment to explore the love again.

Millions of years passed by
Witnessed the Mother Earth from the beginning,
Pledged to create life around you
with body shrouded in mystery,
And fresh air to breathe and blow
For all around.

Rains made you wet like an incessant cry of pleasure
Sun could not enter you more than you needed,
As you took the vow to let the lives on you breathe well
And allow them to grow.

The civilisation grew
Around you and because of you,
Then came the lust in the people
They didn't care for those very hands,
Which held them, with care and love
They cut your arms and legs,
They raped you time and again
You helped them to have strong lungs out of your own
They damaged the same with massive fires,
Miles and miles of your body burned
They failed to see you weep
On your largest water way.

Amazon, my dear
We do not know what we have done,
Help us to get our senses back again
Help us to regain our love for others,
For the sake of every life on the earth,
To allow flowers to bloom as it did in past
for million years till the doomsday
'Father, forgive them, for they know not what they do.'*
And we seek your forgiveness, too.

*Luke 23:24

To My Best Friend These Days

Let me take you to my best friend
A new relation has grown deep in last few days,
A friend in need is a friend indeed
With wide open arms to hug and pray.
Hand in hand, we look at each other
I look at trees outside,
Green leaves waving at me with gentle breeze
Birds flying around,
Cheers in their chirps—talking to each other
Cracking a few jokes, maybe.

Many windows appear from past,
I can see a little barefoot boy with dust in the feet—
Playing games with his friends in a far-away village
with ecstasy and joy as pure it could be,
With the sorrow of failure sometimes
Wandering in the woods alone
The embrace of mother in the hide and seek game.
The dusk sets in
on the deserts of my city,
Hungry virus looking for victims
with blood in its teeth and the dagger in the hand,
Smelling a victory for sure
All the human voices are silent now.

The resolve to fight grows within
Slowly but surely,
Energy transforms in men in black
The fight is to begin soon.
Zeal of will power
Power of pure Sun and Moon,
And a pure world outside
Made from purer hearts.

I touch my friend with stronger grip
Thanks for showing me the world beyond me,
With a stronger hug I embrace—
The friend who stays with me, when alone
The window in my room—the best friend these days.

Lost And Found

A close-friend when I was a child
More and more elusive as years rolled on,
And one day, I could not find you anymore.

Now, I am in a self-made prison cell
Pondering on my deeds and future,
With a little window to look though outside
And wide-open sky with a beautiful hue
With nature dancing in the form of clouds,
You appeared under a veil.

When did I say thank you from the bottom of my heart,
To a house-help or a driver or a staff in the office
Or someone somewhere who helped me?
Did I expect that from others when I grew up
and helped someone higher up?
The apple was good at first bite and made me happy
It did not taste the same after some time,
Even though there was no change till last
Did not care for need to say
I appreciate.

Dear Gratitude,
Now that I have found you again,
Please lift your veil and come back as soon as you can
And take me out from the black hole.

Snow of Kilimanjaro

Woke up in the middle of the night
I had a dream of a black knight,
With a snow-white cap covering half the face
Riding on a Pegasus, ready to fly.

Unable to see the face of the man—
Turned away from me in shadows of cloud,
When moonlight fell on the face
Could not believe that it was me.

Slowly, I sat on my bed
Sweating on a winter night,
As I walked through my door to open balcony
I entered the canvas spread wide.
It was cold outside
Looked at the silver night,
Far behind the stars
I saw the tallest single mountain of the world
Breathing from the mouth of a giant-lizard
After a long time.

I could see Harry walking towards peak
to find the answer to the riddle,
The volcanic crate about to wake up
With Helen looking for him down below
A love of her life lost in time.

Rayli has not snorted for long time
A silent giant is getting up from the sleep,
Flew though sky to the peak on my horse
To stop Harry.

Then the snow started melting down.

Firefly

One night in camp at Serolsar lake
along the Great Himalayan National Park,
Inside the forest in pitch darkness
When the only light was the camp fire,
Around the tents we have lit—
Burning with black oak tree leaves,
a bunch of fireflies came to greet us
with blinking light right through the forest on ravine,
Giving us the signal of life around.

A lone firefly fell in front of me
I picked it up gently and put it in a glass
With a lid on the top,
Still blinking slowly like an unexposed love in a prison cell
Suddenly, my young days came back,
With the first love in my life
I made someone prisoner of my beliefs
And lost her very soon.

With trembling mind and hand
I opened the glass lid
And took out the love bug,
To let it fly again
Far away from me in the zone of love, peace and friendship.

Oskar Schindler

'Whoever saves one life saves the entire world.'
- Talmud (Book of Jewish law)

The engraving was put on a golden ring
Made from the hidden gold filling of the Jews saved,
The love in their eyes when you said goodbye
The passion in the eyes of Helen when she looked at thee.
I can count people like you from the time of history
to withstand the pressure of the brutal force that may be,
Strong enough to lose every penny for the cursed ones around
with a rare kindness in eyes to make the nature cry,
With the reverberation in the oceans of the world.
Gentle breeze whispers in the air 'Oh, Schindler'
Hope mankind has few more people like you.

Dreams

You fly so high and low
Sometimes vanishing in the cloud,
As if to touch the world above
When I feel I have lost you forever,
You come back like a lightening through the sky
Bringing hope once again.

For a child, young or old
You remain a dream forever,
Not knowing what's going to happen to you—
a sad end or as a hero,
with sorrow or happiness at the end.

I wish I could be like you—
float with the eternal time.
Go above the clouds to see the vast spread from end to end,
If there is an end
Changing colours like aurora borealis.

Is a dream to me when you fly
Oh, my favourite kite
People may think you have no life,
How wrong they are as they don't know
You carry my soul in the sky.

Destination Not Known

I saw the carriage in the middle of the night
Looking like an old school bus but small,
The body protruding out in the front
I could see better now—
A vintage carriage with a driver,
Tall, white horses on both sides, raring to go
Driver dressed like a coachman of a Texan movie,
Curved cap and thick moustache, ends hanging down,
Shouting out if anyone needs to go.

The carriage was parked at the end of the road from my house
Tall cedar and pine trees on both sides,
Sky was overcast and could not see much ahead
Except a little crescent of a moon smiling
through the curtains of clouds floating away

The carriage was parked under a streetlight,
Looked like hundred years old, a gas one may be
The pillar carried a road sign with the shape of an arrow,
Somehow could read the words on the same.
Painted black on the wooden plank
Large letter marks “To Anywhere”.

I walked on the path and the carriage was near
Mumbled to myself 'Where to go now?'
Driver waved and called me to come in,
'How much is the charge?' I asked
He smiled and said, 'Don't bother'
No charge for passengers going to Anywhere
It's not meant for others who want to go Nowhere
I had many options but I was muddled,
I still didn't know whcrc to go
Driver shouted, 'Now, it's time to start!'
He could not wait anymore.
With a sudden jerk the carriage started,
I jumped in without knowing where it was going
But I slipped and fell from the door.

Next thing I knew that,
I rolled over from my bed to floor.

One Night At Tapovan

The snowy peaks of Bhagirathi on one side
with Sudarshan behind the masiff,
On the foothold of Shivling Parvat under an ice cap
Mount Meru and Manda giving the company to each other.
The mountain range around the horizon
Holding the greenery on the lap,
Moonlight glitters on the tiny body of Alok Ganga
Flowing through the heart of the valley.
Large glaciers forming the body of holy Ganges below
The little hut of Mounibaba on the way to Nandanvan,
Clear blue sky holds the umbrella from end to end
With the sparkles of moon floating on white clouds,
Flowers blooming to add to the splendour of the moment.

Is it heaven? I mumble to myself
A small sound may break the tranquil peace,
Then, I see that I had no past and future
No one at home or outside at large
An empty man who has nothing to show,
In the large still landscape of a picture frame
From physical body to a tiny fragment
I stand to witness me transform.

Sound

Heard so many sounds in life—
Glacier from mountains into rivers
Ice breaking from an avalanche,
Lava coming out of volcanos
Waves breaking on to shore,
Rainfalls falling on the tiles of the roof
Melodies of Symphony in an opera,
Drops of dew falling from the leaves
Bees flying with the nectar of flowers,
Birds chirping to each other
Animals with diverse sounds,
Hurricanes on the land or sea
Gentle murmur of breeze from the woods.

The different languages people speak in different countries;
Different cities and villages,
The machines in factories
The cars and trains.
A heartfelt laugh or crying in sorrow,
Weeping silently when parents left
For their last journey.

But the best sound in the world—
sound of quiet stillness in a lonely night
when there is only the self as company,
The world around watches in awe
when we talk to ourselves without uttering a single word
experiencing the best sound, we can ever feel.
The sound of absolute silence
that reverberates time and again within,
like a soundless cascade of waterfall.

Dusk

It was a late winter day after sunset
With dry yellow leaves of pine and oak trees on the pathways—
slight brown on the edges,
The park that's big enough to hold a rhapsody of life every day.

The sky starts changing colour from orange, violet
And finally yellow and red
with hues of purple and blue
at moments a little touch of grey,
You came slowly in a chariot for a short journey
wrapped under a veil and a long dark dress.

As you spread the wings of mystery under the sky
Many of us wait for you patiently,
To think of the past and hide our sorrows
To share the darker side of the life.

A young couple in thirties sitting at a distance
with each other
They may have come to the park to come closer,
From the bound of four walls to the wide open
They have grim faces
as if they are not able to manage the distance till now.
Wonder what will happen when they go back,
But I cannot wait
as am in a hurry to see others.

Alone a lady in sixties sitting there
Her face has some wrinkles and worry,
Looking blankly to the trees around
Like a statue from a still era.
And suddenly, I see tears in her eyes
Using her scarf to wipe out the eyes,
Let me move again to another bench
There are some arguments I hear.

The couple in fifties decently dressed
words coming out from the mouth in a louder note,
And they have their hands moving forward time and again
With fingers pointing at each other.

Moving again to a quiet place
Away from sounds that's not a part of nature,
And there is a couple in twenties sitting,
talking to each other in whispering tone.
Smiling and holding hands of each other
Looking some time eye on eye,
Close enough to merge into one.

An elderly couple in eighties
Hand in hand,
One hand of the lady on the cane
Sitting quietly with smiling faces,
Occasionally a few words to express
Reminiscing the old days, maybe.

Then came the voices of children
Smiling from heaven,
running around in a corner
Indifferent to the events around
with no worries for past, present and future
And hope for a better day.

Dusk, you are there to give shelter
To people with sadness and sorrows,
No one can see others under the shadow of your dress
Darker and darker as the time flies—
Unravelling life stories from sealed envelopes.

As I prepare to come back from my walk
Moonlight sparkles on the longer trees,
I see few fresh leaves looking up.

Remembering Ayn Rand

Throughout the centuries few of us took first steps,
down new roads, armed with nothing but their own vision.

Don't ask questions when nobody can answer
The man is made of new ideas,
But the dystopian state goes against it.
The business today is to control the mind
and put the mindless people in lockup for life.
Don't forget what's good or bad by construed confusion
In the spider network of social platforms,
binding them all to a mindless state.

A freedom which is far from true
The mind is corrupt with the use of viral invitations,
Freedom of choice has wrong connotation
Voluntary association is turning to life sentence in a prison,
Individual judgement is controlled by juggernauts
Aristotle, you would be sad to be around.

The reasonings do not exist any more
Man is an ordinary animal of Animal Farm,
Run by the pig-headed pigs
In the grave danger today facing extinction.
Free mind of mankind
In Roark vs Keating duel of ideas,
Roark is losing the game.

John Galt, we need you today
Maybe you can save us from
An impending catastrophe of mankind.

My Childhood Hero

Some said you are one of the greatest kings Bharat ever had
Some said love has acted as your enemy,
Some say that life is not as depicted by popular story.
All I knew is—
You were the favourite King
The tragic hero of my childhood days.

Who can forget your first battle with Muhammad Ghori?
Rendering his first defeat in a fight,
Or your magnanimity to let him go scratch-free
For which you paid dearly in later days.

There are so many romantic stories around the world
Romeo-Juliet or Layla-Majnu,
Cleopatra and Mark Anthony or Paris and Helena
Our own Salim Anarkali or Shahjahan and Mumtaz.
All ended in tragic finish
But they don't match valour of your highness,
You made history live, hijacking a princess you loved
On a secret message sent thousand miles away.
Without the known communication channels of today
I could still hear the sound of galloping horses,
With arms holding the reins and the Princess in arms.

We had many fragmented states
Each fighting war with others,
When enemy was ready to take advantage of the same
You were the face to save Bharat—
Uniting the forces from north to west.

Alas! you fought against greed as always
The story of treachery in our land repeated,
Losing the final battle to the ghastly outsider
The story of the court poet is what I would like to believe
(No matter what historians say).
Depicting the days of your blindness in prison
And your relief with the final sacrifice,
Killing the enemy with an arrow form your bow
With just the sound of target without sight.

Barbaric force made the final entry to our sacred motherland
To form the sultanate,
With you gone
Rai Pithora Prithviraj Chauhan,
the last great King, Bharat had
Before we lost our freedom for a long time.

Joker

Ladies and gentlemen
It's my life,
I live to make you laugh
As you come crying here.
Rest of the time
I am a useless piece of furniture,
Lying in a corner of a house of cards
A listless name in a telephone book.

You fight, you lose, you try to run away
From the problems of life as you come to see me,
To forget the sad memories for sometime
To travel to a different world of jokes and fun.
(Which are silly, by the way)
And I repeat those mindless moments
Difficult? Not really!
Replaying the same tape time and again,
(Actually, an expressly boring matter)
Just for the sake of earning my livelihood
Food and drinks for the next day.

My heart cries, pain in my body and sick is my mind
But you can't see that inside my funny dress,
And comical make up on my face
Painted red from chin to chin,
That's my blood you don't know
Oozes out now and then.

Hey, that's my life
Life of an insignificant man—Hahaha!
Have a nice day!

A Mysterious Legend

One day I was in your court—
You on your massive throne,
With the eminent sword at your side
To protect the sovereign country, you inherited.
Making it the mightiest in your time
Beaten the Saxons and the mysterious enemies,
With supernatural powers
The Excalibur to elevate you as a legend.
Scaring all oppositions to death
Through folklores, stories, dramas and movies,
Written and re-written several times in later days.
That also had another sword of family lineage
Retrieved by breaking a massive stone,
Showing your might to countrymen
'The sword in the stone' to prove the legacy.

I looked at your Royal Advisor
Magician and sage Merlin by your side,
Who helped your father, Uther Pendragon,
To win the fort Titanjel on the peninsular coast.
Surrounded on three sides by turquoise blue water
in the disguise of the King Gorlois,
To win his queen lady Igraine—your father's beloved, too.
You conceived on that dreadful night
of magic, courage and fight.

I looked at Lancelot, Chief Knight, and a personal friend
Who has been with you through all the time,
Who will besiege your wife Guinevere's love
Bringing the end of a colourful reign.

But you lived for ever and ever
In people's mind from childhood to old age,
As the greatest legendary king of Britain
King Arthur of Welsh!

A Migrant Story—Lockdown Days

Walking for past few days on highways, dry land,
bridges and railway tracks;
Young and old, men and women
some pregnant, some holding small children on the back,
Carrying whatever we have in the sacks
With one set of clothes day after day—
Torn in many places,
Worn-out slippers, sometime tied by a twine
Sometime pieces of cloth covering toes or foot itself
With cuts, bruises, blisters and plantar fasciitis—
Blood oozing out.

The day comes with scorching Sun at noon
with no place to sleep at night;
Food or no food, donated or left overs,
drinking water from any source we get on the road.
New born baby looking for milk from mother's dry breast
Just sucking the nipple in lieu of an old habit,
Mother looking at the child not knowing what's to be done.

Don't know how many miles to walk—how many days
Someone tells us as we move,
Which way to go forward, like a herd of cattle on the field
Lucky if we get some transport.
Meeting up demands and bribes
With another journey as livestock in a moving truck,
No cover or toilets on the way—
Fortunate ones may get the train.

You were talking to someone on mobile
With complaint on the quality of life these days,
The boredom and housework for some
Sitting in comfort of a big home
with abundance of food and drinks.
Worrying about boredom and future
How much losses you incurred from job or business,
From the safe haven of your beautiful home.

Did you ever look beyond self?
To think of the people at large,
The migrants who are on the roads 24 hours a day
To find their wives or husbands or fathers or mothers
awaiting eagerly.
To see us at home
Our final destination of thatched roof and clay walls—
What we may never see again?

Wish

I found Aladdin's lamp one night
As I rubbed the lamp on the stone nearby,
The genie came out behind the fumes and smoke.
I could barely make out what it said
With a pleasing smile but a hoarse voice,
I can grant only one wish to you
But I will disappear very soon.
I have exhausted all my grants over the years
This is the last one I am left with,
You need to ask for it now.

I am in a dilemma what to ask,
Should I go for a life-long trip with luxury?
In my own airplane, car and cruise boat
To the destinations I have not been able to visit,
From Amazon to origin of Nile
From north pole to south pole to Siberian desert.

Should I choose to go back to past couple of hundred years?
In Scotland among the clans—
Frasers, Gordons and Mackenzies
Or the Vikings of Nord.
In the time of Lodbrok or Fairhair
Or still further back in past,
Among the Incas in Cusco
With the Sapa King,
Or still back with Mesoamericans during the Mayan rule

In a place like Yucatan,
Or a fast forward to see what the future looks like
On the saucers and the spacecrafts;
Throttle past planet after planet
When life on Earth will cease to exist.

The genie said my time is up
I said hold on please,
I know where to go now—
Please take me back
to my childhood.

Smiles

Its fresh new morning with Sun about to shine
I set my foot for the park nearby,
For a brisk walk meeting fresh old friendly faces
With new hopes and plans for the day.

Men and women walk in groups
Few prefer walking alone;
Some are silent, some with music buds in ears
Some love to talk, some reply when needed,
Women discuss servants and children
Men on politics, starting from national to world issues,
Looks like all the solutions to problems are hidden
inside the garden.

Some give tips on share market
Like wisemen of stock market with great analyst's mind
Some talk on sports—how Virat played a wrong shot
Or how the catch should have been taken;
Few on travelling, science and technology

Most on the news or jokes
Starting with something like psycho-man killing children.
A yogi who duped his disciples
Or a tornado devastating some place,
Sometimes laughter spreading its wings
From one corner to another,
In a corner there is roaring smile from the laughter club
Supposed to give longer lungpower.

Some walk with all the problems of home and world
With a sombre face,
Most of them smile when they see each other
With greetings or simple waving of hands.
The smiles are infectious—quite different during the day
Cannot be classified in the three types we know,
Some like crescents stretching of mouth to cheek
Polite to wistful, some flirtatious ones from opposite sex,
Some of them with Pan Am smile
Like when you enter a flight and see the airhostess.

The best is when you see a Duchene smile
which begins from twinkle in the eyes;
It spreads with subtle violin play on the entire face
And lifts the mood for everyone walking,
The gentle breeze starts blowing from south
The Koyal on the tree tweets with the favourite tune

I look for a sunny day ahead.

Sunshine

Cyrus the great freed all labourers from bondage
Five hundred years before the birth of Christ,
Declaring equal rights for all human being
throughout his vast Kingdom—
From Aegean Sea to Indus River,
The first charter of human rights for mankind.

In our own motherland Bharat
The Great emperor Ashoka transformed after Kalinga War,
Turning to one of the most compassionate King ever
Even set up the first animal hospital—
Two hundred years before the birth of Christ.

We have modern civilized society now
But even today,
Humanity is treated no better than animals
Hospitals inferior to the forest
with greed and bribe;
Only the great nature stands to safeguard the dwellers.

The hungry sharks are lurking in the dark
The wolves are waiting for the smell of blood,
The jackals are out to elude the victims
The rulers remind the story from George Orwell,
In the metamorphosis of some human being
Turning into worse than animals,
We are back to the same world of yesterday.
History repeats in a different form,
Today.

I Want To Breath

(In memory of George Floyd)

There are many hearts which are bleeding in pain
Vast number of souls willing to help,
Unfortunate that they have silent voice
They only mumble among themselves.
Will there be some to come forward?
Fearless and bold—
Uniting the force of anguished observers
To rise against the immoral,
To bring the freedom from discrimination
With the right to life, liberty and security.
Without torture or degrading treatment,
Resisting human being to turn into slaves again.

Someday soon the Sun will shine on all of us
Equally,
There will be a rising for all of us to fight
And bring justicc to humanity
Amen!

Covid 19—Looking Back

Winds of change have blown in last few decades
Passing through a continuous process of switch,
Many times, we forgot who we are—
Withered human bondage,
Raptured social fabric;
Greetings and smiles lost their value.
One by one, new guests came in line
Television, mobile, internet and games;
Gadgets after gadgets, white and black.
The guests sat in our home and became part of family
Ruling our life without any sword or gun,
Like a virus never seen before
Took away the golden moments of our lives—
Togetherness with friends and family.

And then you came
We denied you, got angry, frustrated to final despair;
Before our acceptance for you as a part of our life
Unlike other guests you were the most unwelcome,
To have you as friend turned out to be a social curse
Blocked from all others near and dear.

We all choose our seats in life
Front or back, like for theatre or movies;
Sometime standing at the boundary to watch the flow
And join the show at the opportune moment,
Or like Atlas, we carry the weight of the entire universe
Or we stand on a turtle
Which, if moves,
may shake the entire world above.

We changed ourselves as we grew from childhood
Like two sides of a coin
Losing wonder in our eyes for a little flower blooming
A little bird chirping on the trees
A firefly coming out of darkness
Or a beautiful butterfly evolving from caterpillar,
Obsessed with madness for physical wealth
Burning the values we had in childhood—
Human bondage and true love for each other.

Then you came to our home as the most unsolicited guest of all

Suddenly, we found moments to open old envelops
Carrying long forgotten handwriting of
Parents, brothers and sisters
Cousins, aunts and uncles, far and near friends,
With a throbbing heart what's written inside.
Sometimes smelling the same before opening
Anxiously entering thc hcart of someone else close,
Looking at familiar scripts
Or discovering new ones,
Forgotten treasures of our life.

With lockdown open in phases
Windows will open now one by one,
Doors will open someday to the outside world
Know not whether the world will also change
And the humankind back with love and care for each other.

Oh Father, allow us not to lose your blessings ever in future.

Sangam

Ganges landed from matted dreadlocks of Lord Shiva
To wash the ashes of sixty thousand forefathers of Bhagirath,
Travelling all the way from Mount Bhagirathi in Himalayas
To Bay of Bengal at Gangasagar.
Witness the Ganges merging in the vastness of turbulent water
Waves going back sometimes in her body,
Submitting herself to the endless expand of a mighty sea
After embracing rivers after rivers.
Land after land
And the human being,
Wonders of nature's abundance of creative beauty
Among the tribe called mankind.

Looking at Mount Everest closely from the base
The pẹak touching the cloud and the sky,
Merging into one another
In the abundant space above—
Majestically looking at smallness of us
With timeless abundance of beauty,
A limitless wonder of faceless creator.

Remember days in Isle of sky
Inside an archipelago,
With a tranquil coastline of the peninsula and narrow lochs
Radiating out of a picturesque skyline.
Clouds after clouds touching the mountain and waterbody
Kissing and merging with each other,
May be lost in each other's arms
In an embrace of overflowing joy.

In my small world when I close my eyes
Suddenly, I see a floating image of myself—
From past to present and future
As tiny particle of the whole,
Looking brighter at day time
Gradually dissipatc with final rays of VIBGYOR colours,
Sometimes in a cloudy and sometime in a clear sky.

Before merging in the horizon of eternity
Have I been able to light up others' lives?

Moonwalker

One night, I landed on the moon.

I started float-walking to explore
I see another creature like mine on the way,
Looks like from a different planet
'Where are you from!' He asked me.
(With the help of a language converter.)

Where do I come from! An eternal question for me
Scrambling for the answer, I scratch my head;
Is Earth my address—a small planet on the horizon here!
Or to be specific—Am I from India!
Do I come from a state there—
or the city of Mumbai!
Of a particular house, lane and pin code
Is this my address because I stay there at night—
and sometimes during the day!
Even though I travel in my dreams sleeping or awake.

How do I give my address?
When my mind flies sometimes among Syrian refugees
Running with them to escape the mortars and the guns of the
Warmongers,
Who have their selfish interest above all?
At the cost of bleeding limbless children of God.

Am I like the mercenaries of Dogs of War!
With no permanent address—
To save values, not for money
Bringing down the dictators of the world.
Turkey, Russia or China
Or the iron curtained North Korea,
To salvage the rights of the country-men.

Am I part of the gypsies!
Travelling from one place to another
With black magic and nomadic life,
Meeting different people and people with difference
During my journey.

Do I belong to Arab Bedouins!
Moving with herd in search of green pasture
Hospitality, honesty and courage as the norms for living
Business not at the cost of humanity.

It could even be the opposite,
I belong to a small village in Japan
Where happiness has been the rule of life.
With largest no of Centenarians from
A small village of Okinawa,
Jumping out of the bed with smile and energy as a routine
'Do something' is the way of life.

Or from another life of quietness
Enjoying the company of each other in silence,
Prayer with candles and flowers
From a typical Danish riviera small town,
In Hygge's way of happiness in life—

Do you know your address—my dear friend?

The Key

Where did I lose the key,
and when?

Climbed so many mountains
Travelled long distance in the deserts,
Deep inside the forest, desolate places on the earth—
The seven seas and oceans,
Could not find the key I looked for.

Met so many sages
People of high wisdom,
The brilliant scientists
The high knowledge centres,
Sought the help of friends far and near
Missing the key even then.

Perhaps, in my last journey
On the mountains near Karmabar pass,
Near the border of Afghan and Iran
A Sufi saint singing.
Reaching the high under the open sky with boundless horizon
Full moon in the sky,
Music resonating in the pinnacle of eternity
Reaching the twinkling stars in an endless canvas—
Holding the cosmos with wonders
In true melody of life beyond life.

As he sang the truth of being
Suddenly, I found the key,
That was always with me
I did not have the eyes to see.
It was lost deep inside the garbage
Collected over the years inside me,
On the quest for happiness in wrong routes.

As the truth revealed
At the far end of my journey,
With little time to gather the precious jewels
inside the magical box—
Locked for all these years.

I will still try to touch the jewels
Before the end of my journey,
To be able to enter the new world
of pure earth, water, air, and mind.

Small Boy Bill

Small boy Bill
Trying to walk with blindness,
Not really blind
Putting on his mother's scarf to cover his eyes tightly,
With the help of a neighbour friend.
He cannot see now
Trying to move around in the living room,
Broke the Italian flower vase
Glasses scattered all around.
Stepped on a piece and had a nasty cut on the foot
The door lock clicked,
There were footsteps coming to living room.

In were his parents back from work
Upon hearing the story of Bill,
Who wanted to follow the blind king
his teacher has described from an Indian Epic.
Not at all amusing and out of sense, father and mother said,
'Why, Bill? You are not blind.'
How does Bill tell them that
He wanted to experience the agony of a blind man.

Days go by
Hands tied tightly by the neighbour friend on to chest like he wanted,
Bill has no hands now
Just as the young beggar on the pavement outside school.
Pushing the begging bowl in between legs
Lifting the bowl up when someone puts a coin,
Practicing with the lovely Japanese bowl
A showpiece kept on the couch table.

Unfortunate as it was
The vase broke while pushing,
In came his parents like the other day
An angry father and upset mother.
What the hell is wrong with their crazy little son?
How could Bill explain that it was an experiment
To see the life of a young beggar,
Who does not go to school like him?

Came another day
Again, the neighbour friend helped him to tie the legs back,
Bill had no legs now,
Crawling on the floor like a child beggar,
Trying to touch the feet of passers-by.

Holding the begging bowl in between knees, Bill moves
Alas! Losing the balance tried to hold onto the standing lamp
That turned and broke the window glass,
As it shattered, a large piece pierced through his head
He did not remember things after—
Till he saw his anxious mother
Looking at him in a hospital bed
And the face of a bemused father with a worried face;
'Why, Bill, what makes you to be someone you are not?'
Mumbled Bill, 'Just to be someone less fortunate
That I am not!'

Perhaps a Bill
Living within all of us when we cry,
As we hear the story of some
Unfortunate ones.

Gate Pass

I had a gate pass
A blank white paper when I came,
In this garden of zoe and bios
Crossed million miles, faces;
Through a turbulent period of time
With changing habits and values faster than I could blink.

Came across so many flowers
some beautiful with heavenly fragrance,
Some having either of them
And some having none.
Some soft, some hard and dry
On paths well laid or hardly laid,
Many a times, forgot the way
Lost time to reach there where I want to be.
Be behind by couple of years
Sometimes making a fortune,

Did not know—why was I chosen out to earn a favour?
But quick enough to forget in blaming others,
when I faltered.

The white paper looks greyish now,
Will turn to black gradually, I guess.

The time for searching my soul has arrived.

Hey Man

An abundance of fresh water and air
With lustrous green around you,
Seen you grow from one civilization to another—
Urus to Harappa, Palembang to Bukhara
Alexandria to Rome, Baghdad to Kiev.
Constant prosperity growing in your head
A strong stimulator to drive you to believe,
You can create whatever you want—
A perfect creation in a perfect world,
Reaching moon and mars.

Let me ask you a question—
Have you been able to create a life—
I did?
As a mother to mankind,
I created you all.

You are now killing them slowly and surely
Exploiting what I gave you,
Taking foolish steps to grow faster
Polluting the very air and water given to you to live well.
Floods in Kashmir or Uttarakhand or Yangtze River
Cyclone in Odisha, Earthquake in Izmir, Santa Maria, Haiti
Hurricane Katrina, Andrew, Tohoku
Ice storm in Texas—
Callously forgetting each incidence of disaster day after day,
Moving forward with destruction of
My gift to you,
A foolish man closing his own eyes.

Someday, I pray, you will have your wisdom teeth
Remind you to realise that,
The very growth you are proud of
Is slowly killing your children and grandchildren.
There will be no paradise but hell
With a constant threat to final eclipse,
Due to your own vanity and ignorance.

May you be blessed soon to regain your senses
and the soul I gave,
Restoring nature around you
Amen! Om Shanti!

Loneliness

Alone here
At this moment,
For some moments
How long?
I don't know,
I know sometime from now
I shall turn to dust beautifully—
To wind,
To meet the leaves, flowers, trees and birds.
So many close to us—
Once close to us but left back when time called,
The butterflies may carry some extracts from flowers
to the trees around
That also will be over some day.

Life
You gave me so much
Beyond hate, anger, despair and greed—
Precious moments of love and happiness
Aroma of freshly grown paddy,
Wet soil after rain
Tweets of bird unknown,
Walking on the bank of a smiling river.
So many faces came and gone in the train
Stations passed by one after other,
Noise gradually came down around me.

Loneliness
You wrapped me around in this cold winter morning
like a Pashmina shawl,
In the balcony of my log house
at Kausani hills—overlooking the meadow.
With cows and sheep's grazing lazily
Under the reflection of glitter of morning Sun
From icy peaks of Himalayan mountains,
Sitting alone
At this very moment
here, alone.

My Journey With You

I touched your face with my soft little fingers
Birds sang, winds blown softly,
The kind eyes looking at me.
Love flowing from heaven like drizzle
and then it rained in kisses,
All over me—
From palm to eyes to lips and cheeks
No place left in my body,
Mama, my fingers started the journey with you.

I gripped the ring finger of a strong hand
Surrounding that with all my strength
with complete trust,
I was ready to face the world outside.
A confidence I derived from you
as long as I could hold you with
my fingers wrapped around yours—
Dad, that was my second step.

The fingers found one day a pleasant face
With love in her eyes,
Holding softly but firmly in my palms
A new window of relation was open
to share the joys and pains together,
Owning the responsibility equally.
My fingers had a different impulse,
My journey started with partner of my life.

A day came,
A flower bloomed in the horizon of ours—
A set of soft fingers surrounded mine,
Holding on as I did many years ago.
This time I owned responsibility—
Bestowing the trust and confidence
To a new born,
Entering this world of ours.

I was walking alone in the garden
My fingers wrapped around the head of a walking stick,
Someone greeted me from behind
Like a familiar tune carried by the sound waves
from many years ago.
A little bird tweeted—bringing back memories,
'Where have you been, my dear?
I haven't seen you from a long time.'
Laughing and talking about good old days,
His hand now extended to me
Holding onto the fingers of someone close.
I let the stick go away.
As long as I had friends
I didn't need it anymore.

ABOUT THE AUTHOR

Bidyut Baran Sen is by profession an engineer and has a business of manufacturing speciality chemicals. His personal life has been crafted as a non-conformist with a passion for trekking into high altitudes of the Himalayas, exploring historical monuments and sites across the globe with an interest in photography and piano.

Originally from Kolkata, Bidyut is now settled in Mumbai for the last 40 years. Besides his wife Rina, he has two sons and a granddaughter.

www.ingramcontent.com/pod-product-compliance
Lightning Source LLC
LaVergne TN
LVHW041119150826
845673LV00007B/2125

* 9 7 8 9 3 9 0 8 8 2 3 0 4 *